Don't Take No for an Answer

MATT HUFFMAN

DON'T TAKE NO

FOR AN ANSWER:

THINK YOU CAN'T GET A MORTGAGE?

Think Again.

Don't Take No for an Answer:
Think You Can't Get a Mortgage? Think Again.
Matt Huffman

Printed in the United States of America

First Printing, 2019

ISBN 978-0-9998584-3-1

www.dreamhomeinfo.com

Contents

Chapter 1   7
My Awakening

Chapter 2   15
Stop Making Excuses.
If You Can Afford Rent, You Can Buy.

Chapter 3   25
Why a Broker Loan Officer Instead of a Bank?

Chapter 4   33
Do You Really Need a Monster Down Payment?

Chapter 5   43
Why Buyers Are Denied—Credit

Chapter 6   53
Why Buyers Are Denied—Debt-to-Income Ratio

Chapter 7   65
Why Buyers Are Denied—Assets

Chapter 8   71
Why Buyers Are Denied—Property

Chapter 9   97
Never Accept No for an Answer

Chapter 10   85
Why I Can't Take No for an Answer

About the Author   91

CHAPTER 1

My Awakening

One-third of Americans do not own the home they live in. That means that every month, a staggering 100 million Americans pay someone else's mortgage rather than investing in their own home and financial future. While some people choose to rent, most do so because they don't realize they can qualify for a mortgage. They just need to know what to do, and that's not always obvious, even for people in the mortgage business. People like me.

After working for one of the largest banks in the United States for over five years, I was offered a promotion and transfer to Florida. What an opportunity! I had always wanted to live in Florida. The downside to this offer was that my wife and I had to pack up our home of four years and move in just two weeks! We were so caught up in packing, sorting, and cleaning that we neglected to make living arrangements for when we arrived in Florida. The result was a painful lesson.

When I imagined life in Florida, I saw a home surrounded by gently swaying palm trees, and I'd be lying on a float in our enormous pool with a tropical drink in hand. My wife and I were both excited and nervous when we pulled into our motel in Southwest Florida—me behind the wheel of a 26-foot moving truck with a car hauler; she driving our SUV pulling a 12-foot trailer. We had landed, but now what? We quickly connected with a few realtors over the phone and finally settled on the agent we both liked best.

"Do you have a preapproval?" our realtor asked right off the bat when we called.

Of course, I knew that I would need one, but with the chaos, I had not even thought about it. I logged into one of my credit monitoring services since, due to a bad divorce 12 years prior, I had had to declare bankruptcy. Even though I hadn't really worked at establishing credit since, according to the monitoring service, my score would be fine for getting approved. And I knew my income was fine. Once my wife and I decided on the price range, I called my bank to do my mortgage. (For obvious reasons, I couldn't do this myself as it's considered a conflict of interest.)

To my surprise and chagrin, they told me that my credit score was much lower than what the monitoring service had shown. I was declined without suggestions, help, or guidance.

Now one would think that someone with 16 years of experience as a loan officer would know what it would take to be approved for a mortgage. I did, to a point. What I didn't know is that not all loan officers are created equal. I learned the hard lesson that choosing the wrong loan officer can mean the difference between being approved or denied.

The rules of brokerage loan officers are so much more flexible than those of bank loan officers. Not knowing this caused both my wife and me unnecessary stress that could have easily been avoided. Like us, most consumers think that all loan officers are the same. When they get turned down by a bank, they go to a different bank, not realizing that the banks are all playing by the same rules. They keep getting declined. I will discuss in depth the differences in chapter 3. For now, back to my story.

After suffering this blow to my ego and seeing my dream of buying a new home in Florida shrivel like a day-old balloon, my wife and I were forced to look at renting a home while I worked on raising my credit score to qualify. Unfortunately for us, the cost of renting between November and April in Florida is three times that of the summer months. This period when all the retired people come down to get away from their winters and drive rental prices through the roof is known as *season*. And we were there during *season*.

Since we couldn't afford to pay $3,500 a month rent, we lived out of a motel room where we washed dishes in the same sink where we brushed our teeth. This could have been demoralizing, but I was determined to better our situation. After *season*, we rented a house at $1,400 a month.

My realtor suggested I call her mortgage broker. On tenterhooks, I called James. He pulled up the same score the bank had and approved me. *Say what?* We had just spent two months living in a cramped motel room and then another six months forking over rent.

"So why did the bank say no when you're able to say yes?" I asked.

"Matt, the banks make their guidelines stricter than the brokers do to protect themselves. The program actually only requires a score that's 40 points less than what the banks demand."

Now, I was aware of what are called *overlays*. This is when banks add stricter guidelines to cover their rears. I just didn't know they also did this with credit score requirements. Brokers, on the other hand, don't generally have these overlays.

As I soon would discover, that wasn't the only difference.

"You know, if you pay down one of your credit cards by about $600, that would improve your credit score and would get you a better rate," James told me during one of our phone conversations.

Wow! Bank loan officers, which is what I had been, are prohibited from giving any kind of credit advice.

Additionally, we didn't have access to tools like the credit simulation that James had run for me. It turned out he was right. I followed his advice, and my credit score jumped 68 points.

I was beside myself with excitement. Being a loan officer myself for so long, I had documents to my lenders before they even asked for them. Shockingly, even knowing the process and what to expect, I was a nervous Nelly from start to finish.

After what seemed like an eternity, I finally heard from James. I'll never forget that phone call. It was about 8:30 p.m., and my wife and I were sitting outside by the screened-in pool at our rental house. When the phone rang, I jumped to my feet and put the phone on speaker.

"Hello?" I answered nervously.

"Matt. Hey, it's James. Just got off the phone with the underwriter, and they've given final approval on your application. When would you like to close?"

Chills ran down my body. "Are you serious? It's completely approved and ready to close?"

He confirmed, I thanked him for everything and hung up. "YEESSSS!" I yelled, jumping so high I hit the lanai cage with my hand.

This string of events was a career-altering experience that would ultimately change the direction of my mortgage career forever. I will never forget the feeling of being told *no*, nor the feeling when I was told yes. I vowed to remember the nervousness, anxiety, anger, frustration, embarrassment, and fear followed by the complete and utter thrill of getting final approval and use it all to better understand and serve my clients. That was also what ultimately made me decide to leave the banking world after 16 years and try my hand at the broker-side of lending. Although most of the business was the same, I was about to learn that there were so many people I could help that I couldn't before— more than I ever thought possible. They just have to believe that they can, and should, become homeowners.

CHAPTER 2

Stop Making Excuses. If You Can Afford Rent, You Can Buy.

The national average for rent is $1,445 per month. That means that on average, signing a new lease costs $4,335 with first month, last month, and security deposit, which is often more than it takes to purchase a home. Too often, people wind up renting when they can afford to buy a home simply because they lack the confidence or information to make the decision. That's what happened to Chris.

Chris's lease was about to expire, and he didn't know where he was going to move to. Sarah, one of Chris's family members, is a realtor, and she introduced Chris to me.

"I've been thinking about buying a home but don't know if I can qualify or if I even have enough money," Chris told me when we sat down together.

After hearing his concerns and answering his questions, I said, "Chris, there's a bond program that I think might work for you." He looked at me with a puzzled expression, and I began to explain how the bond programs work.

Bond programs, whether they're run by the county or state, are designed to assist first-time homebuyers with a down payment and closing costs. Depending on the county or state, they can offer from $7,500 - $15,000. We will discuss these programs later in chapter 4.

The next day, Chris filled out my online application and began his home search. When all was said and done, Chris had to pay about $800 out of his own pocket for inspections and appraisal, but the bond covered the down payment, closing cost, and even reimbursed him for the appraisal at closing. He could barely believe that he was suddenly a homeowner.

Fast forward about 18 months: We were recently out on Sarah's boat hanging out at a sandbar. Even though some time had passed, I recognized Chris as he pulled up on his boat.

"I'm loving owning my home," he told me after we had exchanged greetings. "I'm in the process of renovating the kitchen and have several other projects on the horizon."

The pride in his voice was obvious. So was the relief he felt that he was finally investing in himself rather than paying off his landlord's mortgage.

Like many, Chris had never thought about just how much money he was wasting by renting rather than buying. Think about it! If you pay $1,200 a month in rent, every five years, you throw away over $72,000. By the time you put down that first and last month and security deposit, you could have bought a $150,000 home. Obviously, the amount of rent you're paying changes the amount you're throwing away and the home you could afford. But no matter how you look at it, it's a hunk of change.

That's not the only money you're dumping down the drain. A lot of people don't realize that you get to claim up to $10,000 a year in interest as a tax deduction. What does that mean to you? Well, if you're in an 18-percent tax bracket, on top of your standard deduction with the IRS, you get up to another $10,000 off your income tax, putting $150 extra a month back into your pocket instead of in Uncle Sam's.

If I had accepted no for an answer and continued to make excuses and rent, in a five-year period of renting vs. owning, not only would I have wasted approximately $72,000, but I would have lost up to $1,800 a year in IRS savings. It's not just the money that I would have thrown away. I also would have lost the potential equity I would have built in my new home. All of this together would add up to around $94,000 over a five-year term.

Astonishing, right? That's a breakdown of $18,800 a year or $1,566 a month of savings/equity I had been throwing away. And oh yeah, what was your rent? $1,200? Notice that the savings over five years is more than the rent itself? Amazing how we let fear and lack of knowledge impact our finances in such a negative way and not even know it.

That's exactly what happened to Dawn, a very dear friend of mine who actually introduced me to my wife. Long ago,

IF YOU CAN AFFORD RENT, YOU CAN BUY.

Dawn and I lived on the same street of 17 homes in a very small town. I didn't know her personally back then and wouldn't be introduced to her for about 20 more years, but when I was, I remembered seeing her sitting on her porch in her rocking chair, drinking coffee.

I was hanging out with friends in a gas station/deli by day, and karaoke bar by night. The bar was attached to the back of the gas station. Sounds weird, but this place was and still is a very popular locals' hangout.

As I was returning to my buddies from the restroom, Dawn ran over to me and asked, "Do you have a girlfriend or a wife?"

"Uh. No," I answered.

She grabbed my arm and dragged me over to meet the woman who would eventually be my wife. As I was getting to know this woman and Dawn, we figured out we both had lived on the same small dead-end road in a little rural town. Since that time, she and her husband split up, and she moved into an apartment complex, the same one my future wife resided in.

Dawn was a single mom of four boys and didn't think she could qualify for a mortgage. For years, she rented because she didn't see how she would ever save enough money to buy a home. Through our working together, she found out that she could qualify for a bond program that paid her down payment and closing cost. This newfound information prompted her to go house hunting for the first time in over a decade. With the help of the community bond program, she found and qualified for an adorable ranch-style home where she still lives today. Without the bond program, Dawn would still be renting and would be what I call a Terminal Renter.

The Terminal Renter is someone who either chooses to rent or is renting because they don't know they can qualify for a mortgage. Those who say they prefer renting are usually content to stay where they are because they haven't done the math. Perhaps they like the community feel of an apartment complex. But you don't have to sacrifice that when you buy.

For someone who truly likes apartment life, I would suggest a condo. You still have neighbors in close proximity; you have the pool and workout room, among other amenities. You also get the maintenance-free life.

IF YOU CAN AFFORD RENT, YOU CAN BUY.

If a pool and workout room aren't your cup of tea, then I would suggest buying a townhome, in which maintenance is typically covered.

Either way, you're better off buying than renting. But owning is outside of some people's scope, witness one of my assistants.

After a few months of working with us, Meagan mentioned that she was going to look at a condo to rent for $900 a month.

"But, you have a good-paying job now," I said. "You're 19 and can get into a home with little to no money out of pocket. Why not buy for the same or less payment?"

Immediately I saw the wheels in Meagan's head turning, but I also sensed some hesitation.

"I'll think about it and talk it over with my mom tonight," she said. Then she asked that we not say anything to her mom.

I start pulling up some homes in the area Meagan was looking to move to, and lo and behold, we found several options. I could tell she was getting excited. Then ironically,

Meagan's mom, who had never been to our office, walked through the door.

"Mom, I'm going to buy a home!" Meagan instantly blurted out.

So much for contemplating over an evening, I thought. But I was excited for Meagan and eager to help her find that first home.

Meagan looked at several homes and bounced back and forth before making a final decision on which property she was going to select. We ran the numbers on each house so that she would not only have an idea of how much, if any, she would need to pay to close on this house, but also to ensure that she was comfortable with the monthly payment. Once she selected the home she wanted, she put in a contract. It was promptly accepted by the seller.

I had told the agent how much she should ask back from the seller in order to help Meagan with the closing cost. This, along with the bond program we found for her, allowed Meagan to buy the home with no money out of her pocket. Meagan is now a proud new homeowner. But she wouldn't be if we hadn't had the chance to talk. Even though she works in the industry, it just never crossed her mind that she could buy a home. That is exactly the reason for this book. I want everyone to realize their dream of homeownership, even if they don't know it's a dream yet.

As a side note, you certainly don't have to opt for a townhouse or a condo, even if you don't want to spend your weekends mowing the lawn. If you're the type who dreams of the house with the front porch and white picket fence, you can have that and still not have to deal with maintenance. I have paid a landscaper for the past five years. I don't care for yard work, and honestly, it's worth $100 a month to me to pay someone else to take care of it. You can easily justify this expense when you consider the money you're saving on taxes because of the interest you get to deduct. It's all about how you lay things out to yourself.

Sometimes, spending money can save you money. Weird concept I know, but as I've shown, when you break down the numbers, you're actually saving more by owning a home than by renting.

One argument I've heard against owning a home is the cost of maintenance. "Matt, come on. I don't have the money to maintain a house of my own." Of course, I have a counter to that as well. Would you believe me if I told you that 88 percent of Americans knowingly pay monthly for something that will always depreciate, always needs maintenance, and puts their lives at risk every day? You might have figured it out already, but that 88 percent own or lease a vehicle. In fact, the average household owns two cars. You could say the same thing about credit cards. We knowingly apply for and use credit cards generally to pay for things we cannot afford to buy, so we end up paying two to three times more for that stereo we just had to have because of the 18-percent interest we paid for three years. According to NerdWallet, in 2016 the average American household had $16,061 of credit card debt. Let's face it, we've all been programmed to wastefully and irresponsibly spend our money with renting, buying cars, boats, motorcycles, and other toys, and with credit card debt. All that ends up costing you money. A house will absolutely cost you money as well. But unlike a car or credit card debt, the value of your house will most likely appreciate. You just have to decide to make the leap, and then find the person who can help you get that mortgage.

CHAPTER 3

Why a Broker Loan Officer Instead of a Bank?

Given the choice, would you ride a train to work or drive a Ferrari? It may seem an odd comparison, but in my opinion, a bank loan officer's like a train and a brokered loan officer's like a Ferrari.

Let's face it, to keep up with the volume of clients, bank loan officers can only focus on the obvious. They certainly don't have time to investigate alternative options or programs that might be able to help a client. This can leave the client discouraged and feeling hopeless because they've been told they'll need to save a lot of money to purchase the home. As we will see in the next chapter, needing a lot of money to buy a home is a myth.

Lack of time is only one of the issues with bank loan officers. In addition to being over-worked, they're generally only able to move in one direction. They must stay on a specific track and cannot exceed a certain speed, or they'll crash. They're limited to the two or three products that their bank offers, generally cannot offer any financial or credit advice, usually take 45 to 60 days to complete a mortgage loan, and have little to no alternatives to go outside of the box.

By comparison, brokered loan officers are like Ferraris because they have a ton of amenities (i.e., products), are fast (they tend to close in under 30 days), and have a multitude of options to assist with advice, counseling, and products.

When I came to the broker side of the industry, the difference between what I used to do as a bank loan officer and what I began to do blew my mind. Brokered underwriters are empowered to make judgment calls for what I call *make-sense lending*. Let's say you're a borrower with a questionable item on your application or credit, yet you've been at your job a long time and show stability. In most cases we'll overlook that sketchy issue that would otherwise disqualify you with a bank. That's just one of many examples of how the mortgage broker side can and will practice make-sense lending when banks won't. Who you choose as your lender can, unfortunately, dictate not only the experience but whether you are approved or not. Michael discovered that the hard way.

Michael had found his family dream home and wanted to buy it more than he had ever wanted anything. He, his wife, and two kids had been staying with family since moving to Florida and were desperate for their own space. But he was running out of time. Michael had been turned down five times by banks because his debt-to-income ratio was too high (how much he had to pay to cover debts each month compared to his monthly income). He was on his third contract extension, and the seller was going to back out of the contract.

When you're looking to purchase a home, one of the criteria that's considered is how much debt you have compared to how much income you have. Let's say you make $3,000 a month, and your monthly debts total $1,500. The lender will calculate your debt to income at 50 percent even before adding a new mortgage payment. In this case, your qualifying for a mortgage is highly unlikely. But if those debts can be brought under control or repackaged, that will put a different spin on your loan application. In some cases, for example, we can have clients pay off credit cards or other debts to help bring the debt-to-income ratio down to a much safer number.

In Michael's case, he had multiple small credit card balances and installment loans. He had five credit cards, each on which he owed less than $200, but the minimum payment on each was $25 a month. That may not sound like a lot, but getting rid of $25 a month of credit card payments would allow you to qualify for about $5,000 more on a home. By getting Michael to pay off the five credit cards, he eliminated $125 of his monthly debt, which allowed him to qualify for about $25,000 more. That enabled him to purchase the home he wanted.

Granted, brokerages like the one I work for often allow higher debt ratios than banks simply because, as we've seen, the bank puts in added protection for themselves. In this case, however, Michael's debt ratio was still too high even for broker standards. It would have been just as easy for me to turn Michael away as the five previous loan officers had, but my job is to help deserving people get the home they have dreamed about. After reviewing

Michael's application, I started scrambling to figure out the cheapest way to help him get his debt ratio where we needed it to be.

Once I had a clear plan of attack, I instructed him on exactly what cards he needed to pay on and how much to achieve my plan. Michael was able to get a financial gift from his mom and used it to pay the items I had requested. Two days before the closing date, we were able to get Michael's loan back to the underwriter and obtain final approval for the mortgage. When I made the call to Michael to give him the news, the phone fell silent for a few moments. And then, "HELL YES, FINALLY!" Those types of moments give me the most satisfaction in my work – when I get to tell my clients *yes* when so many others have said *no*.

I wish more people realized that bank loan officers only have so much latitude because they must play by the bank's rules – or follow that train track. That is particularly true when it comes to overlays. As we saw in the previous chapter, overlays are guidelines banks add to protect themselves. For example, a bank may say the maximum debt ratio they will allow is 50 percent, but the program actually allows for higher. In this instance you may be denied by a bank when a broker could have approved your application.

That is exactly what happened to Rick. Being a guitarist for a famous and successful rock band, I don't think he's heard many *no*es recently in his life. But he couldn't be a nicer, down-to-earth guy. Due to not being able to obtain a mortgage after age 70 in the UK, he was forced to sell his home there and decided to move to Florida. His income obviously was a little random, depending if he was touring or not. When we met, he was living out of a hotel room with his wife and dog—definitely not an ideal situation. I felt horrible sitting in his hotel room, signing documents on his 70th birthday. Here sat a man whose band is known worldwide, but because of lack of vision from his bank and the loan officer, he was basically homeless. We came up with a game plan and were able to make the deal work. Now he and his wife, and their cute cocker spaniel are living happily in their condo by the beach. Had he continued working with the bank loan officer, they would probably still be sitting in that hotel room.

When I worked at a bank, I was sometimes given as many as 20 clients a day who were seeking a mortgage. As a brokered loan officer, sometimes I go a day or two without having a new client inquiring about a mortgage. What that means for the consumer is generally far more resourcefulness to make as much out of every opportunity and provide a higher level of personal customer service. The bank loan officers are more likely to concentrate on the consumers that do not have issues or hurdles rather than spend time trying to find a way to help someone who may have some issues, something my team excels in and thrives on.

Janna and Jim, a father and daughter, were looking to buy a home to live in together. Jim has early-onset dementia, so this was a complicated process. Sometimes we would need to talk to him ten times a day to re-answer the same questions. It was extremely important for us to make sure he truly understood everything. We achieved this through a lot of due diligence and communication at every step of the way to make sure everyone was informed and understood. Thankfully, Janna was also on the application, by educating her on all facets of each step and explaining every document thoroughly, Janna was able to help answer her dad's questions and concerns, and clarify when he wasn't quite sure on something. In the end, we were able to help Janna and Jim close on their new home. Unfortunately, banks typically would not have taken the time needed to properly handle Jim's situation in this way. Sometimes the difference between a broker and a bank is as simple as spending the extra time and effort to assist clients. Other times, the knowledge that brokers have about programs that can provide down payment assistance and the like can mean the difference between owning a home or not.

CHAPTER 4

Do You Really Need a Monster Down Payment?

If you could buy a home with little to no money, would you? According to the 2018 Millennial Homeownership Report, almost 62 percent of millennials cite the lack of a down payment as the reason they're not buying a home.

Most people think if you don't have money for a down payment, you can't buy a house. As we have seen in Chris's story in chapter 2 and will see with Holly's story, that's just incorrect. With the creation of private mortgage insurance, lenders are more willing to lend with less money down from buyers.

Private mortgage insurance or PMI should not be confused with homeowner's insurance. In almost all cases, when you put less than 20 percent down on your home, you will have to pay PMI. Why? Because if a lender is forced to foreclose on a property, they usually get about 80 percent of the value of the home, so in effect, PMI is an insurance policy for the lender that the homeowner is required to pay.

"How long do I have to pay PMI, and does it automatically go away?" you ask.

The answer is different depending on if you're using Federal Housing Authority (FHA) or conventional financing. FHA will have a mortgage insurance premium, which is basically the same as PMI for seven years, no matter how much you put down on the home. Conventional financing is a little more complicated. When you feel you have reached about 22 percent equity in your home, it's for you to call your lender and request an appraisal that you pay for out of pocket. If you have at least 22 percent equity, then the lender may remove your PMI.

DO YOU REALLY NEED A MONSTER DOWN PAYMENT?

PMI may cost between .5 and 1 percent of your loan amount per year. For example, if your loan amount was $150,000, and you were at 1 percent PMI, that would add $1,500 a year or $125 a month to your mortgage payment.

I know. Bummer. But PMI is often a necessary evil if you want to buy a home and don't have the 20 percent down payment required.

That's not the only option for would-be homebuyers who haven't saved up enough money for a down payment. According to "The Mortgage Report," there are some 2,000 down payment assistance programs nationwide, many run by state, county or city governments. Unfortunately, a lot of people and even loan officers aren't aware of the many different opportunities.

The fact is that with all of the community programs, bonds, grants, and other first-time homebuyer programs, people often get into homes with little to no money out of pocket. The bigger cities have their own programs, but most counties or states also offer similar programs.

Do these programs truly give out free money? If so, what's the catch, right? The type of program you and the lender choose will dictate the conditions of having to repay or not. It is important to know the differences between grants, bonds and government down payment assistance, and why one program may benefit you better than the other. Most do require a credit score of at least 640, have debt-to-income ratio limits as well as income restrictions, and dictate the rates. Although most of these programs are strictly for buyers who haven't owned a home in the past three years, there are also programs out there for people who are not first-time homebuyers.

GRANTS

Holly was looking to buy a home, so naturally, she went to her credit union. She had heard about the community programs, but when she sat down with her credit union, she found out they didn't participate in any. Luckily, a friend who had previously worked with me suggested she call to see what I could offer.

Holly's credit score was great, she had a very good income and enough saved up for her down payment and closing cost, but she wanted to take advantage of a community program. After sitting down with her and researching her options, I suggested the Lee County Own a Home Grant in Florida because she could get a $10,000 grant that she would never have to pay back. With some of the community programs, such as bonds, you pay back when you refinance or sell the property. However, grants are literally free money offered to first-time homebuyers. While the interest rate on Holly's loan was slightly higher than she would have otherwise gotten, this allowed her to buy her new home with very little of her own money and to use the money she had been saving to furnish and decorate.

BOND PROGRAMS

So, what is a bond program, and what are the pros and cons of going with this over a grant? Generally, I use the bond program for loans under $200,000. The reason is that it offers more money than a grant at a lower interest rate on the mortgage. For the purposes of this explanation, I am going to use the Florida Housing Authority Bond as the example. The Florida bond offers $7,500 for qualified first-time homebuyers to use towards closing cost and down payment. The $7,500 is treated as a silent second mortgage that accrues no interest or fees, and requires no payment until you sell or refinance. Then you only pay back the $7,500. If you sell the home, the $7,500 would come out of your proceeds from the sale. If you were to get $10,000 profit from the sale of the home, they would take the $7,500 out leaving you with $2,500 profit. If you refinance, they would just add the $7,500 into your new loan amount and that would take care of the bond.

Some other programs may reduce the amount owed after a certain period. For example, North Carolina Housing has a program that reduces the amount you owe from the second mortgage by 20 percent a year after you've lived in the home for ten years. So after 15 years of owning the home, the second mortgage is forgiven, and you don't repay anything.

As I've said, grants aren't paid back. This is obviously the pro for this program, so what's the con? Grants typically have interest rates on the loan that are .5 to 1 percent higher than the bond because you aren't required to pay the grants back. Grants give a percentage of the loan amount, so if you're borrowing $200,000 and getting a 4 percent grant, your grant would be $8,000. In most cases, I suggest my grant clients refinance in two to four years to a lower interest rate and lower mortgage insurance.

A lot of people ask why banks don't offer down payment assistance programs. The reason is that most banks are generally portfolio lenders. What this means is that they close your loan and keep it, and you always make your payments to them. Most of the down payment assistance programs are serviced by one major lender, so your loan will automatically get sold to this bank no matter who does your mortgage. Since banks are in the business of keeping their loans, they don't offer these programs. That fact almost prevented Laura from being able to buy a house.

Laura had tried to get her mortgage with her bank, but because they didn't participate with the community program she had qualified for, they couldn't approve her application. The community program was giving her $15,000 to use for the down payment and closing costs. Because brokers are typically set up with the local community programs, we were able to get her approved using the community grant. Even with down payment assistance programs, knowing which program will work for your borrower is imperative, as we will learn in the next story about Deo.

Deo had tried to buy a home with a couple of banks and even a couple of brokers. He had a great income, but he hadn't been able to save enough to buy a home. He was working three jobs just to make ends meet. After being turned down by the banks, he took a shot with a local broker. The broker attempted to get him qualified for a down payment assistance program, but unfortunately the broker was using the wrong program. Different programs have different requirements. The one the broker had tried to use required tax returns for anyone living in the house, even if they weren't on the application. Deo and his fiancé combined made too much money to qualify for the program. One of my realtors, Julia, told him he really needed to talk to me.

When we met, I could tell he was skeptical. After some reassurance, he agreed to try the application one more time. During the process, he committed one of the major mortgage sins and opened a credit card to buy his fiancé her wedding dress. When he told me what he'd done, I did the unthinkable. Yep, I made him take the dress back. I definitely wasn't the fiancé's favorite person at that time.

I remember getting word that he was approved and had moved to closing like it was yesterday. Even though I knew Deo was getting precious sleep between his jobs, I called to give him the news. He picked up the phone immediately.

"What's wrong?" he asked.

When I gave him the good news, he fell silent. Then I heard a loud screech of excitement and sobs of joy and relief. After closing, he went back and bought back his fiancé's dress, and they are now happily married in their new home. And his wife doesn't hate me.

Mortgage brokers like me succeed or fail on their reputation and ability to get loans closed. If you can't get loans closed, the client doesn't get their home and has potentially lost thousands of dollars. That's why it's imperative that your loan officer always do their due diligence and know both their products and clients. Confidence, not cockiness, is key. I've been in the mortgage industry for almost two decades, and I know I don't know everything and never will. I also know that if I don't know the answer, I know where to go or who to ask to get the information I need. Every day I run into a new situation. It's part of what makes this job so challenging and enjoyable to me. On the other hand, there are plenty of constants, which anyone can learn to sidestep or address.

CHAPTER 5

Why Buyers Are Denied— Credit

"What does my credit score need to be to qualify for a mortgage?" is a question that almost everyone asks me.

There is no simple answer because some lenders and most banks have their own minimal allowed credit scores. Most brokers like me don't have these overlays. We go by whatever the program dictates. Federal Housing Authority will allow a 550-credit score with 10 percent down payments or a 580 credit score with 3.5 percent down. Conventional financing requires a 620. The United States Department of Agriculture (USDA) has no minimum credit score, but most brokers require at least a 640. On the other hand, some like mine, only need a 580. The Veterans Administration (VA) actually doesn't have a minimal credit score, but generally speaking, a 580-credit score is needed. There are cases where the VA will allow a lower score with compensating factors like a low debt-to-income ratio, down payment, or having a lot of assets. Often, if your broker loan officer is resourceful, they take certain actions that a bank loan officer may not have thought of.

Jason and his wife wanted to purchase a family home that they had been renting for years but had been declined by several banks due to having a credit score well below 580. Since the house was being offered to them for much less than its market value, I suggested that we raise the purchase price from $85,000 to $100,000 and then have his family give him a gift of $15,000 to use as a down payment. Effectively the mortgage amount didn't change, but the process changed the loan to value. Essentially instead of Jason trying to borrow 100 percent of $85,000, now he would be only borrowing 85 percent of $100,000. Since his family would be gifting him the $15,000 towards the down payment, neither the amount of money Jason was paying nor how much his family was getting from the sale of the home changed at all. The system approved Jason and his wife's application despite their low credit score because it saw an 85 percent loan to value as a much lower risk than a 100 percent loan. It's just semantics I know, but sometimes it's all in how you structure a loan.

Credit is the most important piece that will determine if you are denied or approved for a mortgage application. Not only does your credit worthiness affect your ability to qualify, but it can also affect the amount of money you need for your down payment as well as your interest rate. On a conventional mortgage, a 740-credit score compared to a 620 score will get a 1.5 percent better interest rate and you will spend $2,956 less in fees on a $200,000 mortgage. The 740-credit score mortgage payment would also be $184 a month cheaper. Over the life of the loan this amounts to more than $66,000.

How can you save that kind of money? By improving your credit score. Paying your bills on time helps bring up your score. Conversely, keeping high balances on your credit cards is one of the biggest things that bring down your credit score.

Randy was turned down multiple times from various banks. Once again, this was simply a case of where banks set their own rules above and beyond government guidelines – those overlays. Even though the FHA guideline states that we need a 580-credit score, he was told no because his credit score didn't meet the bank's 620 requirement. Since we, as brokers, don't have these overlays, it was an easy deal to get approved.

In addition, there are several actions that can sometimes bring your credit score up in a matter of days instead of weeks or months. Brokers like me have simulators that can predict how certain actions will help get a credit score up at no cost to the client. With these simulators, for example, we can see if adding a credit card or authorized user will affect your score. By being added to someone's credit card as an authorized user, you actually adopt the history of that person's credit card not just from the time they added you, but since it was opened. My dad added me on his credit card as an authorized user several years ago. It reported to my credit with the complete history of the card, which had been opened when I was three years old. That gave me a very long credit history, which helped my credit score go up.

We can also see if paying down card balances or paying off collections will raise or lower your score. If we do come up with a way for you to improve your credit score, sometimes we can even perform what we call a rapid rescore, which will update your paying a balance down or off in three to five days rather than waiting up to 45 days to post to your credit. Jack was one of my clients who took advantage of being added to his wife's credit card to give him an excellent credit score.

When I met Jack, he had been turned down at a bank because he didn't have a credit score. He had never opened a credit line in his life. This isn't ideal. As a broker, I didn't have to have a credit score to get Jack approved for a mortgage, but it would've made the task easier. So, I asked Jack to have his wife add him to one of her credit cards as an authorized user. Two weeks later, Jack called me.

"I've been monitoring my credit like you said, and I think I have a credit score now," he said.

I re-pulled his credit and lo and behold his score had gone from zero to a 792. With this, we ran him through underwriting, and a few seconds later, we had an automated approval that we wouldn't have gotten without a credit score. On top of that, Jack's interest rate dropped a whole percent bringing his payment down over $100 a month.

Another example where I used the authorized user was with Bill and his wife, Ellen. Bill and his wife were sick of the freezing Ohio winters and were determined to move to Florida as soon as possible. After a consultation, I inputted his information. Unfortunately, his credit score was about 50 points away from qualifying for a mortgage. Like with Jack, I suggested that he ask a family member to add him to a credit card as an authorized user. A few weeks later he called and asked me to re-pull his credit to see where he was. It was clear that the new card had hit his credit. His credit score had increased by 56 points, which in turn, allowed me to get him an approval.

Just like with Bill and Jack, I always strongly suggest that my clients allow me to run my simulators before taking any actions on their credit. Sometimes you can take action, and instead of helping your score, you decrease it. I see this a lot, especially with collections.

What you may not know is that in most cases, paying off collections can hurt your score. Collections and charge-offs will stay on your credit for seven years, no matter if you pay them off or not. When a client pays on a collection that is older, it restarts the seven-year clock, so typically paying them is not a good idea.

WHY BUYERS ARE DENIED-CREDIT

If you're disputing anything on your credit, STOP IT. Disputing items, even if they are valid, is a waste of time if you don't have the proper documentation to prove that it was reported in error. There are credible credit repair companies out there who can help fix mistakes on your credit, but not many. I've found that most of them charge several hundreds of dollars for very little to no productive results to your credit. In fact, their efforts or yours on this front can prove detrimental since this also can create a false credit score, which, once the lender has it removed, could affect your qualifying.

Things do happen that you cannot control. I was working with two sisters who wanted to buy the home they had been renting. We were only a week from closing when we found out that a few months before, they had been hit by a drunk driver totaling the car. They expected the insurance to cover the car, but it only covered a portion of what they owed. Not only did they have a balance on a car they couldn't even use, but the financial company reported them late on the payments rendering them ineligible for financing. Even though this was in no part my clients' fault, it's an example of how sometimes events beyond your control can impact your home purchase. I was able to get them on a payment plan and back on track. Even though they lost the home they had been renting, they are now happy owners of another home. I strongly urge that you speak to a professional before taking any action to your credit, especially when closing credit accounts.

Closing accounts is a common issue. When you close a credit card with a balance, it will directly impact your credit score. Let's say you had a $5,000 credit limit, and you had a balance of $1,000 when you closed the account. Since you no longer have an available credit limit, you are now 1,000 percent above your credit line. This could impact your credit score as much as 100 points. That's exactly what happened to my client Matt.

Matt had a credit card that had been charged off and closed. Once they charged off his card, they added a bunch of junk fees on the balance, so even though his credit limit was only $500 on the card, they reported his balance as $900. That meant he was effectively 180 percent over the limit. I had him settle the account with the creditor. That alone brought his credit score up 67 points.

Applying for new credit is probably the worst offense. Buyers often think that once we've pulled their credit score, they're good to go get that store card and buy furniture for their new home or get that new car. But that's one of the worst things you can do.

We always pull a Gap report about a week before closing to make sure the client hasn't gotten any new credit or debts. A Gap report shows the lender what or if anything has been changed since your credit originally was pulled, hence the term "Gap." That's what we did with Cole, who was just days away from closing on his first-ever home. When we ran his Gap report, we discovered he had opened a new credit card since we had originally pulled his credit. Luckily, he had not used the card, so the report showed a zero balance. If he had used the card, that balance could have resulted in his debt ratio being too high to qualify for the home. That's another big piece of the home-loan puzzle.

CHAPTER 6

Why Buyers Are Denied—
Debt-to-Income Ratio

Do you struggle to make ends meet? If the answer is yes, then you should ask yourself a few questions and be brutally honest.

Are you spending money before you make it by buying electronics or other goods on credit cards or loans?

Do you have a budget? More importantly, do you follow that budget?

Are you carrying balances on credit cards and only making minimum payments?

Do you know what your interest rates are on all your debts?

These are questions you need to answer in order to plan to pay down or pay off debts.

First, you need to figure out your debt-to-income ratio (DTI). That's easy. Just divide all your monthly debt payments by your gross monthly income. Too much debt relative to how much money you bring in every month creates a DTI problem.

Fortunately, DTI issues can be resolved by paying down or paying off credit cards or installment loans. They can also be corrected by putting more money down or paying to get a lower interest rate on your mortgage.

Many people ask me, "What's the maximum DTI allowed?" Federal Housing Authority or FHA has the most lenient DTI at 57 percent maximum. Conventional financing is a bit more conservative at 50 percent maximum. The United States Department of Agriculture (USDA) is the most conservative at generally 43 percent maximum DTI. The Veterans Administration (VA) technically does not have a maximum; it takes into consideration your compensating factors such as credit score and assets as Brian soon learned.

Brian was a fellow veteran who was sent to me because his VA application was declined by another lender for excessive debt ratio. Unlike most of the mortgage programs, the Veteran Administration (VA) doesn't have a set debt ratio limit. Because of the different rules and guidelines for VA loans, however, a lot of lenders either steer away from them or unknowingly structure the loan incorrectly, causing a good loan to sometimes be declined.

In Brian's case, his wife also was working, making about the same income as he, but her credit score wasn't high enough to be on the application. Even though his wife wasn't on the loan, I collected her income information and added it to the file. I also saw that he had three installment debts that were expiring in the next few months. I went to underwriting and asked for an exception to ignore those installment debts since they were soon ending. Even though we couldn't technically use the wife's income, having proof of the wife's income made the underwriter comfortable enough to approve the exception. Sometimes it's as simple as asking. And, it always helps when you have extra documentation that strengthens your case.

Despite what some may think, figuring out your DTI isn't rocket science. Take your income before taxes or deductions and multiply by 57 or 50 percent depending on the program. The figure you get is the maximum payment you can have, including the payment of the new home.

If you work full time at $10 per hour, for example, it would look like this:

$10 x 40hr = $400 per week.

$400 x 52 weeks = $20,800

$20,800 ÷ by 12 months = $1,733 per month

Now take the $1,733 and multiply the maximum DTI percentage allowed.

If we're looking at an FHA, $1,733 x .57 = $988 is your maximum allowed payment, including the new mortgage.

Let's say you had a car payment of $250, a credit card payment of $35, and the taxes and insurance on your $80,000 home were estimated to be $568. You would add all of these together. As long as the total doesn't exceed the $988, then your DTI is okay.

So:

$250+$35+568 = $853

That's less than the max allowed of $988. Hurray, you would qualify!

There are things that a loan officer can sometimes do to circumvent debt ratio issues. When a debt ratio issue arises and the spouse/partner isn't on the loan, I sometimes have the non-borrowing spouse/partner put one of the debts in their name instead of the borrowing spouse/partner's. This helps with the debt ratio. When I was buying my own home, for example, I had my wife refinance the car out of my name and into hers to help my debt ratio. Unfortunately, we then can't use the non-borrowing individual's income for consideration for the loan, but I have found ways to use them elsewhere if needed.

Wesley and his wife had been married a little over a year and were expecting their first child. They wanted to have a stable home to bring their newborn to as well as have a place to build their family memories. Unfortunately, Wesley was turned down during the middle of the process of his bank application. His debt ratio exceeded the bank's guideline of no more than 50 percent debt ratio. FHA allows up to 57 percent. We were able to get his debt ratio under the FHA guideline by paying off some small credit cards and buying down the mortgage rate enough for him to qualify.

If your gross monthly income is $2,000, that means the bank will lower your ability to qualify by up to $200 a month. That may not seem like much, but that is about $40,000 of a mortgage. If you're looking at a house that's $220,000, the bank may only qualify you to purchase $180,000, whereas a mortgage broker would allow for the full $220,000. There's a pretty big difference between the two price points of homes. It could just be location, size, or amenities like a pool. Banks are also known to have overlays when it comes to previous foreclosures, short sales, and bankruptcies.

Often these things are caused by no fault of your own. Especially in these cases, you want someone who can look in the "gray areas" to understand your situation and determine that indeed, this wasn't your fault. A bank is generally not going to go down that path with you. They'll decline and move on to the next.

WHY BUYERS ARE DENIED-DEBT-TO-INCOME RATIO

I recently had a deal where the divorce judge ordered the ex-wife to be responsible for the mortgage, and she also got the home. Out of spite, the ex-wife refused to make the house payments and let the home go into foreclosure. Obviously, the ex-husband had no control or responsibility in the eyes of the law, but that didn't stop the creditor from putting it on his credit. In this case, we were able to prove that he was not at fault and got him an approval for his new mortgage.

Student loan debt can also impact debt ratio in a major way.

Student loans are becoming one of the biggest reasons people are denied a mortgage for the home they want to purchase. It surprises a lot of clients how their student loans affect their ability to qualify for a mortgage.

Growing up, my parents pounded into me and my brother's head that you study hard, make good grades, go to college, find a good job, and after 30 years or more, you retire. What they either failed to mention or realize was the exorbitant cost associated with colleges that now requires some seven million Americans to pay for their college education with student loans. Those loans have financial repercussions down the line.

A real estate website PropertyShark, which surveyed more than 2,100 renters and people living at home with family, found that over 35 percent of millennials said the number one reason for not being able to buy a home was student debt.

Except for the Veterans Administration or VA loans for Veterans, all loan products have a mandatory minimum of 1 percent payment calculation even if your student loan is deferred. That means if you owe $40,000 on a student loan that is deferred, the mortgage company will calculate a payment of $400. This can wreak havoc on your debt ratio.

Fortunately, there can be a way around this. In most cases, we have the client take the loan out of deferral, which typically brings the payment down to half of what we would have had to use to calculate the payment. If we use an interest rate of 3.5 percent with a loan balance of $40,000, the minimum monthly payment would be $286 a month compared to $400 if the lender uses 1 percent because the student loan was deferred. That's $136 a month less, which would equate roughly to being able to qualify for about $25,000 more home.

When I met with Gary, he had about $40,000 of deferred student loans. We called all of the student loans and found out what the minimum payment would be if he were to come out of deferment. Collectively, the payment ended up being $225, which was $175 less than the lender is required to use if the loans are deferred. This allowed Gary to qualify for a $35,000 higher home price than had his loan remained deferred.

A lot of young people are getting student loans to go to college but have no idea of the financial strain they are signing themselves up for. And I mean a lot of people! I was talking with Dawna, one of our company's underwriters, about the student loan epidemic we have in the United States. In most cases, the amount of debt a student acquires if they are solely paying for their education with student loans is more than they will even make in a year once they are out of college. According to debt.org, the total U.S. student debt is more than 1.4 trillion. The average student debt in 2017 was $37,172, with about $2,858 of student loan debt being accrued every second. Currently, most states don't mandate any education about student loans, although lawmakers have been discussing bring it into high schools across the nation.

Most individuals who sign up for student loans aren't aware that they largely cannot be included in a bankruptcy or charge off. Today, most student loans can and will levy your bank accounts or paychecks, and there's nothing you can do to stop this from happening except by paying the loans on time or continuing to defer them. Deferring student loans, although often necessary for people who cannot afford the payments, only makes the problem worse. By deferring a $35,000 student loan or loans with an average interest rate of over 5.5 percent will increase what you owe by $1,995 a year. Over five years, your once $35,000 balance will be closer to $50,000, which impacts the amount of home qualify for by at least $60,000. In this example, instead of being able to buy a $115,000 home, you would only qualify for a $55,000 home.

As previously mentioned, the rules are different for VA buyers. If the student loan is deferred at least 12 months past the closing date, we do not have to factor in any payment. That certainly helped out Carrie and Melissa, both former military who had recently married. The newlyweds were looking to purchase their first home together using their VA benefits. Carrie was finishing up her master's degree, and as you can imagine carried a lot of student loan debt. Since she would be pursuing her doctorate the following semester and had already signed up for classes, she was able to get her almost $100,000 of student loans deferred an additional 18 months. As a result, we didn't have to include her student loans in their debt ratio.

Without the VA allowing this, the couple would not have qualified for this home that they wanted so badly. Instead, they were able to close on their home, and Carrie is now working on her doctorate.

Although student loans and debt ratio can be huge hurdles to overcome, having the money, or as we are about to learn, having enough money or assets and reserves is also paramount.

CHAPTER 7
Why Buyers Are Denied—Assets

Homebuyers are often declined for not having enough assets. In other words, they don't have enough money. Assets are generally used to pay for what are called pre-paids, e.g., the down payment, closing costs, and funds for your escrow, which includes taxes and homeowner's insurance. They can also be used to pay down or pay off items on credit to lower the debt to income or to help get their credit score higher.

People who don't use down payment assistant programs must have assets. According to a survey conducted by the real estate website PropertyShark, 30 percent of those surveyed named lack of down payment as a reason they couldn't buy.

A down payment is the amount the lender requires you to pay out of pocket. For example, if you are doing an FHA loan, you must put 3.5 percent down of the purchase price of the home from your own funds or down payment assistance. So, if you're buying a $100,000 home, your down payment would be $3,500. On top of the down payment, you must consider closing costs, escrows, and reserves. I will discuss the fundamental differences between these three in the following paragraphs.

CLOSING COSTS

Closing costs generally are fees that go to the lender and third parties such as the appraiser, closing attorney, surveyor, and the county and state for taxes on the home. When you're negotiating a contract to purchase a home, you can ask the seller to pay a portion of your closing cost.

ESCROWS

Then there are prepaids that are a different part of closing costs. Prepaids are funds collected by the lender to pay for your homeowners' insurance and your taxes. Typically, you must pay a full year of insurance upfront plus a couple of months for reserves. For taxes, you generally pay for the months you will own the home until the next bill comes due. So, if you buy a home in July, and taxes are due in November, you would pay five months upfront. After closing, the taxes and insurance are included in your monthly payment, also known as *escrows*, which the mortgage company pays for you going forward.

Sometimes you're also required to have reserves.

RESERVES

I can already hear you. "I have my funds for closing and escrow, but now the lender wants me to have even more funds. Why?"

Let me explain. Reserves are assets such as savings, 401k, or stock accounts that aren't actually used. They merely show that you have enough money in savings to make up to three payments if needed. In short, reserves are designed to protect the applicant. Should an emergency arise, having reserve would allow you to still make your mortgage payment.

In contrast to assets (the actual funds you need for your down payment and or closing costs), you aren't required to remove reserve funds from the account, just to verify them. Maria is an example of someone I worked with who needed reserves.

Maria had been hospitalized for a few weeks after being in a car accident that was no fault of her own. When she couldn't pay some of the medical bills, her credit score dropped. Medical collections—or any kind of collections for that matter—will do that to your credit. Even though most lenders don't care about medical collections, they can still affect your credit score. Luckily, Maria's score was high enough that she still qualified for the mortgage she needed. However, because of the lowered score, she had to have at least three months of the mortgage payment in reserves to qualify.

As in most things, there are multiple avenues to achieve a goal, even when it's not the traditional way. John and Maria found that out.

I had grown up with John's wife, Maria, and we were friends on social media. She happened to see one of my posts about mortgages and decided to reach out to me.

John and Maria were living in John's mother's home while caring for her. Due to her declining health and mounting medical costs, they wanted to purchase her home. Unfortunately, they didn't have the credit score or assets to qualify for a mortgage. It turned out that John had been added on as an authorized user to a family member's credit card, and that person hadn't made the payments, and the card had been charged-off. With my simulators, I figured out that if we removed him from this card, his credit score would increase enough for him to qualify.

I've talked a lot about not having enough assets. I haven't yet mentioned that you have to have the right kind of assets too. Additionally, those assets need to be deposited in the right way so that lenders can see a paper trail of all deposits that aren't direct deposited. No matter who you're seeking your mortgage with, you cannot just take cash from under your mattress, deposit it in the bank and not expect the lender to ask where the deposit came from. Indeed, they have to ask. It's part of the U.S. Patriot Act.

Why would the government have passed such a law? The biggest reason is to stop money laundering. Let's say a terrorist or drug dealer has a lot of cash that they obtained illegally. In the past, they would buy a home with the cash and then sell it, which meant they could then show the validity of the money. This is also known as washing cash. It hides the true origination of the money.

Okay. You've got everything in proper order. Nothing can go wrong at this point, right? Wrong. There's one more potential hurdle.

CHAPTER 8

Why Buyers Are Denied— Property

The property itself is probably the least common reason buyers are denied mortgages, but it can happen. For starters, property types can come into play, with the different properties that lenders deal with all having their various nuances.

SINGLE-FAMILY HOMES

Single-family homes are the most common homes we see. These are what we call *stick-built* homes. Depending on where you live, they could also include block homes, which are popular in Florida. Single-family homes have the fewest restrictions of the property types.

MULTI-FAMILY HOMES

There are also multi-family homes that are constructed the same way but are often attached. These are generally called townhomes, assuming you only own one of the properties. In some cases, you can have two to four attached homes, which are called a duplex, assuming a single person owns all of them. All the above homes are built on site and are not prefabricated in a warehouse like modular or manufactured homes.

MODULAR AND MANUFACTURED HOMES

Modular homes are built in a warehouse like manufactured houses. The key difference is modular homes are not regulated by the Housing of Urban Development. Instead, they're regulated the same as for single-family homes and must conform to local and state codes. Manufactured homes, as we'll see in the next paragraph, have a few differences.

Manufactured homes, also known as mobile homes, often provide a lower cost option for homeownership. They are made in a warehouse on a chassis, much like an RV is made. Then they are delivered by tractor-trailer to your property. Most people don't realize that when mobile homes are delivered, they are titled just like a car is titled. For a cash buyer, this isn't a problem. The issues with manufactured homes come when someone is trying to obtain financing.

Lenders consider manufactured homes a higher risk. As a result, they have several requirements in order to lend. Manufactured homes must be taken off the chassis and put on a permanent, typically brick, foundation. Then the structure is tied down to the foundation. When buying a mobile home, the buyer should expect to incur an extra cost because lenders require an engineer to come out and inspect that the home is properly secured.

While mobile homes are often more affordable than stick structures, it can be tough to find financing for them. Rob and Amanda, another childhood friend of mine, had been living with Rob's father for the previous couple of years to allow them to save up to buy a home. With their family growing over the years, they wanted to find their own place for themselves and their four kids. Since the homes where they were looking at were so expensive, they decided to purchase a mobile home. However, due to added risk, their credit score didn't qualify them for a $90,000 mobile home. Ironically, I was able to approve them to buy a $200,000 single family home because the risk factor on a standard home is much less than on a mobile home.

CONDOS

Another less expensive route to homeownership is opting for a condo, which is a lot like an apartment, except you can own the unit. They sell for less than traditional homes because you don't own the land, and there are a lot of owners in the same building. As previously discussed, one major benefit of condo living is that you'll often enjoy amenities such as a community pool, weight room, and sometimes even restaurants on the premises. Another benefit is that you do no exterior maintenance like painting or yard work. To those who have busy lives or aren't able to do maintenance or yard work, another benefit is that exterior maintenance is taken care of. Of course, that doesn't come for free. Condos are managed by Homeowner Associations or HOAs. The HOAs charge fees that can be wide-ranging depending on the amenities offered. Some charge monthly while others charge quarterly, but this expense is also something you must consider in your total payment because the lender will include that amount in your debt ratio.

PROPERTY CONDITION

Now that we've covered the different types of property that you may come across, we should discuss an issue that, while not common, can cause your mortgage application to be denied: the condition of the property.

Different programs have standards for a home's condition.

I was trying to do an FHA mortgage for one of my clients, and there were issues with the property that the Federal Housing Authority (FHA) will not allow. In this case, we changed programs and were able to get them approved.

It is imperative that the property you are buying is not only up to the physical standards required by the mortgage program you are using, but also satisfies local rules and regulations. Sandra and Dave were attempting to purchase a vacation home in Florida. They were the perfect clients and seemed like an easy loan. During the inspection period, we found out the deceased husband of the seller had purchased five different lots and built the house in the middle of those properties. There was an error when he filed his will, and one of the parcels had been left out. Of course, the one that was left out was where half of the house had been built. It took a few months, but we were able to get probate court to fix the deeds so that Sandra and Dave could finally close on their vacation home.

The condition of the property can also jeopardize the loan. Nicole almost lost the loan for her house when the inspection revealed that the fence was old and dilapidated. They had planned to take the fence down but had hesitated since half of it was on the neighbor's property. With the mortgage hanging in the balance, they quit hesitating and tore it down. After they removed the fence, the neighbor, whose property the fence was on, called the police and wanted to press charges for vandalism. Fortunately, the police were able to talk some sense into him.

That wasn't the only hitch. When we got her husband's driver's license, it said he was a female. Well, we were in 2018, so that didn't surprise me. He had checked male on the application, so we had to verify which was the correct gender. I called his wife.

"I have a difficult question to ask," I said.

She paused. "Okay."

"Was your husband born a male or female?"

"Umm, I'm sorry," she replied. "What did you say?

I asked again.

A male, of course," she answered. "Why would you ask me that?"

I told her about the driver's license, and she busted out laughing. We all did. When she asked him about the situation, it turned out that he was aware of the error and had just been too lazy to change it.

In the end, we were able to get his license and the home fixed, and they now are happy homeowners. Not sure how happy the neighbor is, but we hope they were able to mend the fence. Pun intended.

As in life, some things are not always easy and don't always make sense. We've all heard the phrase, "where there's a will, there's a way." In the next chapter, you'll see that this is a phrase that I have always lived by.

CHAPTER 9

Never Accept No for an Answer

Anyone can own a home. Really. So many times, I run into clients that are about to or have already given up hope of owning a home. This all stems from being told *no*, but that is something I never tell anyone. I do, however, sometimes have to tell people *not right now*. In these instances, we set up a plan to improve their credit score, save more money, or whatever their specific case may be. Often, finding a solution isn't as clear cut as you might think. Sometimes it takes figuring out a plan and sticking to it.

We humans are hard-wired to get the answers we want. Even a two-year-old doesn't like being told no. I've always been the type when someone tells me no, I am even more determined to get what I want. What I want in my work is to secure you a mortgage, and I don't stop until that happens. Just because you may not qualify for a home today doesn't mean that if you have someone willing to take the time and energy to help you navigate your speed bump, you won't eventually buy a home. You will. You can.

Some fixes are easier than others. One of the more difficult but completely committed individuals I've ever worked with was Jeremy.

Jeremy was a young man who had been turned down by several lenders. He just needed guidance and someone to walk him through the steps. Okay, he needed a lot of guidance.

Jeremy owned his own landscaping business and wanted to buy a home with land where he could store his trucks, trailers, and other equipment for his business. But we had a problem. He was a self-employed borrower who had not filed his taxes for the previous year. I explained that he would need to file his taxes and show at least the same amount of income or more than the previous year. He also needed quite a bit of money in assets for closing that he didn't have when we first met. Over the next several months, he was able to get multiple clients on an annual plan for his services, and they paid him a year in advance. This gave him the assets he needed.

One problem down, one to go.

Jeremy followed my instructions and filed his taxes. Even though his returns showed far more income than the previous year, his accountant wrote off even more, making it look like his income was declining. Once I explained to this wouldn't work for him, he promptly amended his return.

At that point, the underwriter figured that Jeremy was bolstering his return to qualify for the home. In a way, he was, but if he was paying the taxes and that's what he filed with the IRS, and they accepted it, then so should we. Or so I thought. The underwriter didn't agree with me. I ended up escalating the file to our credit committee – basically the "underwriting gods". They initially sided with the underwriter's decision. Me, not being the type to take no for an answer pushed back and got the chief credit officer involved, who overturned the decision in our favor.

After almost two months of back and forth and fighting for Jeremy, we were able to close on his home.

Not too long ago, I called Jeremy. An appraiser for a house I was hoping to fund was requesting that trees be trimmed away, and I wanted to see if he wanted the job. Even though it had been some time, you could still hear the excitement and pride in his voice. He told me he had since bought the lots around his home and that he and his wife enjoyed sitting on their front porch watching the sunsets. That made all the work to get them into that house worthwhile.

Take Richard for example. He had been turned down for a new mortgage by a bank because he still owned a home with his ex-wife. During the divorce proceedings, the court ordered that the ex-wife got the house and was responsible for making the mortgage payments until she could refinance it out of Richard's name and into hers alone. She had, so far, ignored the order. Instead, whether out of financial troubles or out of spite, she allowed the house to go into foreclosure, which went on Richard's record. Most people think lenders just look at credit, but we also pull what's called a fraud report, which has things that even your credit doesn't because it uses many resources, including court and county records. Even though the foreclosure didn't show up on Richard's credit, it was found on his fraud report, and the bank, in turn, denied his application. We were able to provide the supporting documents that proved it wasn't his responsibility, and that he shouldn't be held at fault. To further complicate things, his current wife had assets but had a recent bankruptcy, so we could not put her on the application. By overcoming these obstacles, Richard and his new wife were able to close on their home.

I hope that through the information and examples I've provided, I've managed to convince you that it's always possible to buy a home. If you've been thinking about buying a home, feeling nervous about the process, or if you've already tried getting financing and have been declined by a bank or broker, perhaps some of the tips and tricks I've provided will help. And, of course, if you have more questions or feel I might be able to help, don't hesitate to get in touch.

CHAPTER 10

Why I Can't Take No for an Answer

I've always said if my job were easy, everyone would be doing it. But even those who are doing it, are they doing it well? With multiple different laws and regulations that are constantly changing, it isn't simple to stay on top of changes and on top of all the programs. The job requires keeping a constant eye on what's happening in the industry, being a good researcher, and keeping lots of balls in the air simultaneously. But the most important thing is refusing to take no for an answer.

When I was in basic training in the U.S. Air Force, I was accepted into a Special Op's group called TACP or Tactical Air Control Party. About halfway through my training, my grandfather passed away. I, of course, left to go to his funeral. When I returned, I discovered that they were washing me back a class—basically, sending me back a grade. I was devastated. Through the grueling training, I had built relationships with my fellow trainees, who by then I viewed as brothers. I had to start all over with a whole new group of guys. I struggled at first and sought guidance from our first sergeant. He told me maybe I wasn't cut out for TACP. I wasn't sure if he was serious or just challenging me, but about two months later, I graduated. Even at that stage in my life, the word no and the word failure just weren't an option.

Hard work, determination, and the drive to do everything to the best of my abilities was drilled into me by my parents. My dad always said, "If you're going to do something, you do it right the first time." I grew up on a small farm, about 40 minutes outside of Charlotte, NC. We had horses, chickens, goats, and cows on 12 acres. I had to feed and water the farm animals and collect eggs from the hen house. Most weekends we spent putting up or mending the fences, cutting down trees, or dragging and burning brush and logs from downed trees on the property. My brother and I used to joke that our parents had kids so they could get help with the chores.

I'll never forget when the devastation of Hurricane Hugo in 1989 reached over 400 miles inland to our small town. The storm hissed and whistled through the night and pounded our home and farm. At daylight, when the eye and the worst of the storm had passed, I stepped outside. My parents had a huge bell mounted on a six-foot post that they would ring to alert my brother and me that it was time to come home. When I walked out, I saw that the trees in the yard almost covered the bell and the post. We spent three days from sunup to sundown, cutting and dragging trees, just to make it out of our driveway.

Those early life experiences combined help me to become the husband, father and loan officer I am today. The military also helped build character, determination to never quit, integrity, pride, and honor. All that influences how I do my job.

In short, I'm very much the product of my parents. They were raised in moderate to low-income families in a rural town in Southern Illinois. Though they were both brought up in very strict households, they had very different upbringings. My dad's family lived in the same home for most of his life whereas my mom's family was constantly relocating. I remember her telling me stories of coming home from school to an empty home. While she was at school my grandpa had packed up the house and moved. She would sit on the front porch working on her homework until they came and got her later that day.

My grandfather on my dad's side was very stern but fair. My grandfather on my mom's side was stern, over-protective, and a bit controlling. My parents dated since they were 13 years old on and off through high school and college. After college, my parents wanted to get married, but my mom's father forbade it. By then, Dad had moved to the Charlotte, North Carolina area where he sometimes worked as many as three jobs at once. My mom decided to move to North Carolina with my dad and made sure that my grandpa didn't know. So they eloped and got married.

Although my grandfather didn't like taking no for an answer, this was one battle he wasn't going to win. The path set before my parents was long and difficult, but they were determined to make it together no matter the odds. At one point, they were so broke my dad borrowed $5 from his dad to buy mac and cheese for the week. But they also had been brought up to keep fighting and not give up, and not to accept no for an answer. They both worked hard, well past the time my brother and I were off building our careers and families. Together they have retired to the small farm that I grew up on and are still madly in love well over 50 years later.

I guess you can say I've come from a long line of stubbornness or hard-headedness. That's probably true, but I love the challenge of fixing things others can't—taking a problem apart and reverse engineering it to figure out a solution. To me, nothing is more satisfying. This knack is very handy in the mortgage industry and allows me to better serve my clients' needs.

I've never liked being told no. Most people don't, but in every facet of my life, if you tell me no, I'm going to find a way to make it a yes. That's especially true when it comes to mortgages. There is no other feeling I know of in the world than telling someone they are approved to purchase their home. Owning a home is more than a lifestyle. It comes packed with pride, joy and new dreams. And I'm determined to help as many people as I can to become educated about the homebuying process and to purchase their next dream home.

So I have one question. Are you ready to finally own a home? Then it's time to make that happen.

Matt Huffman

Contact Information: www.dreamhomeinfo.com

About the Author

Matt Huffman was born and raised in the Charlotte, NC area. After his service in the military, he moved back home and started his mortgage career. Some 15 years later, he and his wife, Christi, moved to Florida, which changed his perspective about the mortgage industry and took his business to new heights.

Matt started in the mortgage industry in the early 2000s as a compliance assistant. After working his way into processing mortgage loans, he earned his loan officer license and began to originate mortgages not only in retail but also in wholesale.

Matt spent nearly 17 years working for different banks as a mortgage loan officer before leaving his job as a producing branch manager at one of the largest banks in the U.S. to join the broker world of lending. After a year of working as a loan officer for a broker, he moved up to producing branch manager. While he still originates mortgages, he also manages several other loan officers and production staff.

With almost two decades of experience in the mortgage industry as a senior loan officer and a producing branch manager, Matt has worked with homebuyers to complete over 2,000 mortgages in over 40 different states. More than half of those clients didn't initially believe they could get approved for a mortgage.

During his career, Matt has originated well over $400 million in mortgage loans. Because of his experience, perseverance, and his refusal to take no for an answer, he has helped over 1,000 clients buy a home who were previously turned down.

Matt and Christi now live and work in southwest Florida. Combined, they have over 30 years of mortgage experience. While one might imagine them regularly taking time to romp on the sandy, sunny beaches of Florida, they might get there once a week. They both love what they do and can be more often found in their office.

Matt Huffman

Contact Information: www.dreamhomeinfo.com